millennYELL

millennYELL:

diatribes of self-discovery

Bryan D. Wright

Published by:
Historia|Research Press
Chicago, IL 60605

ISBN: 978-0-9996788-5-5

For there ain't nobody like you

CONTENTS

Foreword

In 2018, Pew Research Center adopted a definition of the millennial generation as persons born between 1981 and 1996. As adults, millennials in the United States have been most closely identified with the term, hope, a nod to their influence in electing the first Black male president in American history in 2008. After the election of Donald Trump to the U.S. presidency in 2016 and a resurgence of white supremacy among all generations, however, the progressive influence of millennials on previous generations or American politics in general has come into question as a transitory or nominal aberration. Recently, millennials have been identified with diminishing lifetime opportunities and affluence due to crushing college student loan debt and the two most severe world recessions since the Great Depression.

The collection of poems herein is intended to complicate the characterization of millennials as naively hopeful or as helplessly impotent. In early adulthood,

millennials have inherited a litany of
social injustices and national crises
created and bequeathed to them by
earlier generations. Domestic and
foreign terrorism, overseas conflicts
and wars, police brutality and
unaccountability, economic distress
and uncertainty, conservative and
white supremacist authoritarianism,
prescription drug abuse and overdoses,
cisgender and heteronormative
chauvinism, and school shootings have
populated the national historical
context in which millennials have come
of age.

In these circumstances, "existing
already, given and transmitted from
the past," millennials have confronted
the traditional torments of self-
discovery and human agency in early
adulthood. In their struggle to make
their own history, millennials have
given birth or nurtured third-wave
feminism, Black Lives Matter, social
media influencers, the occupy
movement, a Green New Deal, and a
revitalized belief in democratic
socialism. Their consumer choices and
preferences have created new cultural
phenomena such as hip-hop crossover
artists, online dating, gender
fluidity and body positivity, *Harry*

Potter, and a renewed faith in social activism and community organizing.

Bryan D. Wright's poems are presented under four main themes of self-discovery - nihilism, longing, despair, and promise - each separated by a timeline of related events in American history from 1990 to 2020. His poetry grapples with key adversities for human agency that face the last generation of the twentieth century: the tenuous grounds on which human meaning and action rest, the risks associated with desiring something over nothing, the anxiety that accompanies the pursuit of goals and values, and the latent (and dismal) prospect for success at the outset of every lifetime of endeavor. His collection of poems - disquieting, exacting, and poignant - intends to express key moments in the emotional turmoil accompanying a prolonged inner dialog on the will to cope with the meaning of adulthood at the dawn of a new millennium.

Historia|Research Press

pRelUDE

PrOEM

I spit delirious
shit is serious
when I'm releasin' it.

Increasin' it, now I'm peacin' it.

Curious still?

I'll show you power of the will.

BDW

niHilism

Gulf War — **1990**

Rodney King beating by police recorded

First abortion doctor killed (Dr. David Gunn)

Waco standoff
World Trade Center bombing

Oklahoma City bombing

Centennial Olympic Park bombing

Heaven's Gate religious group mass suicide

Pres. Bill Clinton impeached

Y2K Bug fears

2000

September 11 attacks
Afghanistan War

Invasion of Iraq (Iraq War)

"Mission Accomplished"

"Operation Streamline"

Hurricane Katrina

College student loan debt grows to $500 billion

The Great Recession (2007-09)

2010

Osama Bin Laden killed

Trayvon Martin homicide by George Zimmerman

Michael Brown homicide by Ferguson police

College student loan debt surpasses $1 trillion

Russia interferes in US election

Trump Sworn in as President

College student loan debt reaches $1.5 trillion

George Floyd murdered by Minneapolis police — **2020**

Breonna Taylor homicide by Louisville police

aGoRAPHobIC

A self-appointed exile,
once more I remain,
imprisoned.

Peering from dark windows
into blinding light
solace in self-pity
sanctuary in sadness
I have remained constant
a war silently raging,
as a single drop
of falling water, in
a stagnant pool.

The ripple propels
beyond its scope,
for only a time,
as waves return silent
and peace reigns until
the inevitable bubble
fills once more only
to disturb again.

The cycle repeats.

rEal LEGacY

It is easy to forget at the bottom of
a bottle.

How much you forget and for how long
is the tricky part.

For what should we remember in the
end?

A life of ease? A life of struggle?

A life that is full or a life wanting?

All is for naught, honestly, in the
final throes of oblivion.

But an essence of self can, in theory,
linger on.

By striving for immortality through
works of art, public service, science
and, in a sense, our offspring.

The latter being the easiest since you
only have to engage in a natural human
behavior. Funny isn't it,
that we can literally fuck ourselves
towards immortality, in a sense, just
through ovulation and ejaculation, two
basic inherent functions of an average

human body.

Woe be to those that have not
accumulated enough to be able to
engage in any of said activities.

That is a true sense of death, isn't
it?

To have no real legacy in some form?

To be truly forgotten?

It is to be erased from the passage of
time,
like a skipping stone that merely sank
into the waters.

I can think of no greater punishment,
torture or hell than such.

fAuX prISon

I find myself beneath the sun's rays.
A brief escape from the self-imposed
exile of "home." The assumed dark has
been my custom and eyes struggle to
adjust to the bright majesty of the
glare, yet the skin-deep warmth is
relieving and cloudless, sky blue a
sight to behold. The passage of time
seems lost between four walls and
within such, my strength always leaves
me but here, I feel renewed but alien.
A sad state to be sure but nonetheless
fact when one is hidden from the world
with only street lights, slurred
banter and stumbled gait that becomes
the norm. A world I am not accustomed
to but calls to me as it once did in
youth awaits just outside the door.
The flies find me an enticing scent.
Unbathed and reeking of foul food and
drink as they dine upon my wretched
visage. My lone cigarette the only
thing that keeps them at bay but it
burns too quickly, and its cancerous
sublime length leaves too soon leaving
me alone with the only beings that
seem to flock to my being. Left with
no choice but to return once more to
my shelter, sanctuary, and prison.

Suicidal vANITY

A constant state of escape
words and emotions lost
in a self-perpetual spiral
towards oblivion.

An architect of my own design
lost amidst the waves shallowly
constructed
and ultimately abused.

I wander towards a certain yet unknown
end, forgotten between faux friends
and mere acquaintances.

Misfortunate spell corrections and
self-absorbed camera shots.

We have lost one another ironically in
a search for one other.

We cannot speak in a world so vain and
have no emotions left to weigh unless
it be some self-satisfying form of
congratulations only made present to
ourselves.

ONLY VANITY
no words to describe
too imbibed.

You are a mess, reverting to a stage
of adolescence unmatched by your peers
and rewriting aspects of a man.

A vain sort of self-importance exists
in which a perpetual loneliness in an
interconnected world.

The words written, imbibed and
ultimately self-serving and growing
less legible.

A selfish shill, meanderings of the
English language becoming so trite and
useless that only faux friends call
them art.

A self-deluded alcoholic state,
ultimately, a lie.

The point self-serving and without any
meaning or contribution.

Just Done.

emBARrassed

Snow falling silent.
more rain than snow.
The sleet mixture hits
my face, propelled forward
by the chill February breeze.
It's early, sun just came up
for a brief moment, only
to be covered in a blanket
of cumulous dark grey.

I wander the uneven sidewalks,
littered with mulch and strewn
with plastic bags floating along
the direction of the wind.
Broken glass and plastic bottles
nestled between city-planted shrubs
and the occasional trampled paper
made unrecognizable
by a length of stampeding feet.

As the sleet becomes more like snow,
I find myself at a familiar door,
in order to evade the weather
I tell myself, justifying my return.
Sitting down once more, upon
a wood table top so well known
I feel if looked I could find my
initials or other evidence of my
passage.

A friendly face asks my desire and thusly grants it, already knowing my reply.

The phone rings, after only three sips, I let it ring a few more times, as I make my way to the door, slightly embarrassed about my location. It is much too early for a place like this. A short redundant conversation ensues with your usual suspects. "Yes" "No" "uh-huh" "that's cool, ending finally with the "alright, you too."

I return once more to my beloved wood table top, the stool still warm and imbibe a strong swig instead. Lack of food helps the medicine go down quicker but tolerance and lack of funds ensures that I won't be too medicated by my departure. Time moves much too slowly, a slight sort of déjà vu brought on by familiar films and music, probably because I'd heard and seen it once before in a state of stupor.

BlackOUT

Sweat, regret,
booze, and drunkenness.

It's not an easy life
the life of a drunkard.

Soft stools, fast friends,
meaningless in friendships
noteworthy respect of
reciprocating and
forgotten memories.

Waking up each day
as a newborn detective
sleuthing through events
and witnesses to the prior
evenings eventual inevitable ends.

Seeking truth of actions and
statements
lost amidst the slandered slur of
friendships cast aside and banal
banter gone
wrong amidst misanthropic
misadventures.

Sweet child in liquors embrace of
frothy dreams
lost and whiskey-laden injuries
sustained.

Either inept and shy or impetuous and
extroverted
you thrive on liquid stamina to
associate with
others.

In a society awry, you wonder how
alone you truly are adrift through
time's passage.

Don't they see the apocalypse ahead or
the banality of existence, the moot
point of survival of the fittest?

I guess we trudge forward into
experience.

niGhtmare AWoKen

I woke up again,
my sleep shattered.
Awaking to silence,
four shadowed walls,
dimly lit, surround.
A subtle glow emits
from the television.
The blue hue blends
into the darkness.
A sinister shade
reminiscent of moonless
nights. I roll on
the bed, towards a light,
fumbling in the dark
my eyes only now
adjusted to the enveloping
gloom. I pause,
weakly scanning, for
sleep's spell still holds
strong, the littered
garments flung throughout...

antAGONism

Slothful penetrating realization
dawns,
unsanctimonious in its wake befitting
the surrounding decay
that autumn beckons. A festering
wound that continues to pucker and
pus,
if only we could prevent the need to
remove the healing shroud of skin.
Trapped within the perpetual purgatory
of self-induced antagonism, the
pitiful
few grasp at self-awareness, to
feel it melt through crease-woven
fingers.
A sharp finger prick that
draws little blood but stings for
hours.
The broken shard of minute glass we
can
never find on our person to pull out.
It lingers there still, becoming one
with ourself.
An aloof, self-sustaining wound,
constant in presence
but evasive of conscious action and
thought.

PASsage of TIME

I lost you through a dark passage of
time, you still exist forever in a
fraction of mind. Ever constant
presence, fueling fantasies of
reunification.

A seldom sort of sobering reality
eluded by intoxicating bereaving
banality. A broken aspect unwanted yet
demanding. A primal, feudal fact
reprised in a self-satisfied, carnal
recovery.

Faces meld to form a surreal ellipse,
a punctuated point of waking that is
constantly matched by self-induced
narcolepsy of the spirit. Ever the
escapist.

The Blind Woman of Scales, should have
borne a scythe. The inevitable failing
of equality, a burden worn by the
guilty, selfish few. You can't escape
the inherent irony of sloth born of
ignorance.

A dove strikes a window. We weep, but
the world moves on, trudging forward
into the abyss of damnation and
delirium.

siREn's CALL

An oral fixation, imbibed at the bar.

Wooden flat top, lined with measured
finite glasses of yellow, brown,
black.

Shades of silver, tan, red and
translucent nectars, that fill the air
with a sticky sweetness.

An alcoholic fumigation that surrounds
all, intoxicating by nature and
alluring in effect.

A siren call, beckoning forth the
unsuspecting into entranced half-
conscious oblivion.

In a waking state of undefined clarity
trudging forth in the ever-open arms
of release.

A never-ending surreal entrapment of
our own making. A dream becomes a
nightmare only to elucidate that we
never really dream at all.

A retreat into self-induced escapism
only to mask…

pasS OuT

Slothfully struggle to the end
of the line fully awake but not
consciousness, too imbibed.

A constant state of being, but
not really alive. A shock to my
system, a host to be revived.

Whiskey and beer you've been too kind,
too a part of my life, you need to be
redefined.

Is it a selfish realization of
machinating mundane? Or a self-pity
that I strive to maintain?

Combinations of both, mathematically
equivalent. I need to sit down the
possibilities too relevant.

A trifle, dirty kind of self-loathing
when awareness made clear but a drink
still holding. Numb to the fact, but
still I wade on, falling face first
into a coma, unable to respond.

I pluck the petals of life's flower.
They blow in the wind as I whisper
truth's name.

It eludes myself, grasping rapidly for
answers. Yet truth exists in actions
not questions.

A realm of reality, complete in
control, that wanes with each denial
of self. Contained by the wicked, mad,
and lazy, the latter reserved a true
place in hell.

SINgle burNING

I stand before the jury as a
man repentant.

A crime, no rosary will soothe and no
punishment just.

I stand before the jury as a man lost.
Lost in a sea of uncertainty,
drifting endlessly, lifelessly amongst
the wreckage of my vessel Answers.

The bobbing questions remind
what could have been.

And continue to remind me what I've
lost.

A lingering flame remains, a single
burning beacon
in the night sky crying, shouting for
attention.

To be noticed by more than one lonely
soul adrift.

As if to summon down the one star that
guided us here.

The star that loved us and led us and
made us

believe in the fabled new world of
bliss
only to be hidden now beyond sight
amidst the clouds.

A fate almost too cruel to bear.

dreadFULLY unSPENT

We shelf the demons of desires wake,
waiting for the self-awaking bliss of
exorcism.

It comes too late, only to find a
pustule mass
of liver rotten, blackened fallacy.

To whom does the bell toll,
tolling endlessly to those driven
towards destruction, a melody of life
dreadfully unspent.

A deeper darkness
with tears woefully spent but no
hand to wipe way.

Such is the way.

The way of self-induced hardship
the way of memory lost
the way of melodic discontent
the sound of fatalistic discontent.

A cadence of wanting
never knowing of what is spoken,
we trudge forward, drink in hand
to all one oppressing oblivion of
sanity, sanitation,
salvation, towards inevitable end.

sLOTH's bROKEn ChRYsalis

Fall ramblings with drink in hand.

Alone again,
I struggle with both pen and
conversation.

Finding solace in action is only the
appearance of normalcy
surrounded by banal banter
no inherent process of thought
all is lost in a whiskey laden,
beer-soaked stagnancy of current days.

No broken cycle. No nirvana found.
Days become weeks, as weeks become
unknown.

Self-delusions of grandeur,
apparent but unwelcome.

The hospitality of body over spirit.
Mind is no master. Matter is the only
true substance.

Three imbibed. Make it four.
I've no home to go.

Stream of consciousness erupts,
as if a forceful Pompeii.

A bad bluff in the face of experts
sunglasses hid nothing;
only mask the insecurity of action
action well-meaning,
but superimposed in a fraudulent way.

Where is our savior now?

Unresponsive and endlessly bleeding,
the life of our sins. Who's to know
what's next in the grand plot.

Elderly machinations put forth long
before birth. We need only act our
designed roles.

The failure, the fool, the peasant-
servant. All found in a shadowy
forward of perception.

Have you my change sir? The constant
irony of such abounds. Change within,
but never change.

A miscarriage of metamorphosis. Still-
born in a state of moribund
fascination.

No butterfly. No moth. A maggot making
due. The world regurgitates a feast.

I am happy to take. No need to find my
own. The path already chosen. The

trails non-existent.

A mud-stream hell of frozen inaction.
Entrapping and suffocating. The
quicksand of illegitimacy. A haunted
past with no present, and a certain
future.

Comfort at last. Inadequacy in
answers. Motivation the cause. Vanity
the reason.

No solution in mind.

Half pASt TEn

I wake up early in the morning
a cigarette still lit in hand
guess I didn't sleep too long
whiskey breath and bottle still on
mind

I stumble to the door now
feels like I've crossed a hall
feet move on their own accord
a falling sort of shuffle
proves I can't stand

man, it's half past ten
I'll be at work on time today
I can't start my car though
it looks like I will be late again
I'm at work now
boss says "where you been"
"trying to start my car"

huNtErs' moON

I find solace in the solitude
escapism evident through
        alcohol consumption.

Seeking to quiet my
pessimistic demons,
releasing ignorant
        joviality.

No solutions to
        selfish issues.

The beerhall sanctuary,
my noisome silence,
drowning the inner
dialogue between
ideal and actual
        selves.

Accomplishment
is subjective
and the voices
of those unsatisfied
whine and wail of
mundane machinations
with little or no
applications,
like barking
bitches calling
for the tug of

a tight leash;
I am happy
        to grant.

Self-doubt caresses
        the surface of all actions.

Coming and returning like
tides on a seemingly
serene shoreline
battered by black,
dirty sludge infested
waters, damned moon,
shining, negligent of
cause and uncaring,
brightly beaming but
        absent of worth.

The black eye of
the sun, only worthy
of being plucked from
its socket with
        anger, fury, rage.

Let none answer the
call of these fallen,
for happiness wanes,
like fresh flowers wilt,
a festering slow decay
that turns beauties
        into blind bastards.

raiNstORM

insanity
fueled by a cloud of drunkenness
demeaning thoughts
the isolated raindrops
found before the storm
blooms
in a perpetual state
of smothering gloom
bone-biting wind blows
down the remaining structure
of sanity
banality found constant
underfoot in the soft
soaked mud

1Onging

1990

"'No' Means 'No'" Movement

Third Wave Feminism

Match.com founded

Friends first episode airs

The Infamous released
by Mobb Deep

Jagged Little Pill released
by Alanis Morissette

Will and Grace first
episode airs

Yahoo! Messenger released

2000

Donnie Darko premieres

57% college-goers are female

*Queer Eye for the Straight
Guy* first episode airs

The Office (US) first
episode airs

iPhone released

Lady Gaga releases
The Fame/The Fame Monster

Grindr launched

2010   Instagram /
Snapchat launched

"Sexting" added to
Merriam-Webster Dictionary

"Selfie" added to
Merriam-Webster Dictionary

Tinder launched

Equal protection for
same-sex marriages

TikTok launched

The #MeToo Movement

'Ghosting' added to
Merriam-Webster dictionary

2020   COVID-19 Pandemic

deFeATEd

I got this black widow baby
she been treating me wrong
got a black widow baby
lord, she been treating me wrong
ain't nothing in this world worse
than a black widow woman you wrong.
She used to say such sweet things
her words dripped pure honey,
straight of the comb.
Now this woman goes around town just
doing wrong,
she's shown her true self,
a spindly shadow thing.

With words like honey, she
tricks the unknown would be.
Full of tact and guile, no greater
conquest I have had, but in the
end I was defeated by no less than the
love I shared.
There is a lesson in all things
good that never lasts,
give your heart fully,
because nothing ever lasts,
and if you should run
across a black widow woman,
just let that shit pass.

Sweet syrup sayings
poured out that mouth of yours,

little did I know that
was just a venom,
slowly seeping into my pores.
Your shallow hidden web
is nothing but a trap laid bare.
I am stuck like a
fly, just hanging around
in there.

I am a selfish,
shallow creature, but lord
knows I try. I am a
selfish shallow creature baby
but at least I tried.
Give love a chance and it bites
you like a dog.

CULTure

We live in a culture of want.

Our desires catered through infinite
desires.

I cry for affection,
but the love shown is not enough,
how selfish it seems but live to our
needs,
we need more than just a friend but
the world to see our faults and flaws.

To comment on supercilious
information.

Trouble in the sea of narcissism,
spelled wrong and spoken inadequately,
love becomes a feeling for a moment,
words illegible, written in distress.

INsomnia'S lONGing

stagnation,
still promises
amongst shallow
waters, rising
and ebbing amid
selfish tides.
muddied waters
of warm embraces
used to keep me
still into the night.
as the ocean still
froths, I long for some
sweet last release from
the presence of moon's
every constant.
only to wallow in the
the fallacy of
seeing you again.
I delude myself
in order for some
self-righteous need to
please, that it wasn't I
that sullied so much
between us,
ultimately knowing
you were always right.
to find something in
one so unworthy
is not much a sin
but a blessing in

a cheap disguise.
that doesn't discount
the diagnoses apparent
but just know its
lacking of merit.
love is a feeling
both sadness and
unwilling, shifting
endlessly between
fascinations. yours,
however, is worthy of
memory, for it keeps
me up at night.

LOve's REspite

You found the last vestige
of warmth in one left cold
wiping away dried tears
and submerging me
breathlessly into
the lake of baptismal bliss
gladly showing no
resistance, I remain
drowned by seafoam
emerald pools that once
knew an obscure aspect
of my worth never
known to myself or
at least hidden away
until your song
awoke it.

Love is but a fleeting moment
that lasts a lifetime
bringing both sadness
and joy and being
both directed and wild
an endless shifting
sea of fascination
at its discovery
yet yours will always be worthy of
memory
for it lingers in my dreams at night.

Ever in my dreams at night

ever in my dreams through the night
yet yours will always be
worthy of memory
it already lingers
ever in my dreams through the night.

A STIll boRn

I saw you in a dream.

Again you haunt my mind
with your ever-present
soul, still trapped within
my conscience, like the drone
of war drums in the night
or the wolf pack howl that
answers its own call
in the lonesome, dead dark.

A shallow selfish thing
to dream upon you still
but the mind conjures what
it most desires through
the blissful sweet release
of memories constraints.

Beautiful creature
you remain still
despite mistreatment by
your delicately wrathful
hands.

Both loving and full
[of acid]
you rend me asunder with
your lack of shared compassion.

A mutually destructive rendering

of two like spirits.

A stillborn birth that
the world weeps.

eLectric rIVErS

Intoxicated atop the hill
looking down at a sprawling
scene of creation

Ingenuity
astounding and life's capacity
to thrive illuminating

Thousands
of little cars pass on winding
highways,
crisscrossing and flowing as if
on electric rivers of machinery

lONEly anyMORE

I've been walking down this long road
dark city alley
and I don't know where it goes
slim city alley
no knowing where it goes
could be my woman
or my maker at the end
who really ever knows
sometimes,
you've got to be hard in this world
sometimes,
that's all you got in this world
but that's a sad place to be
stuck in a way of life that
unfortunately,
not good looking
ragged and dirty too
always been lonely baby
blues only woman been true
won't you stick
stick around with me
I know I don't got much
just my sweet, sweet
company

depRAVEd hoLiday

you are a special sort of
hallucination
a recurring nightmare tinged with the
exuberance
of a flying fantasy, one in which I'm
falling,
spiraling ever downward into your open
arms.

Becoming a pustule stain on your
beckoning blouse,
perhaps only so that you'd remove it.

A recovering pervert, I used to be
perfect, but hell, we all wane in a
certain season.

Bits of me in your hair as you run
those comely little fingers through,
shedding myself like dandruff flakes
on the floor.

A bad taste in your mouth, bitter
sweet on the tongue
and a spice on your lips as you wipe
away,
erasing me as a sensation but the
memory lingers.

Memory lasts only as long as the one

who keeps it.

Your conscious is a twisted beautiful
thing,
wrapped like a ribboned gift but only
containing coal.

No Christmas exists for the callous
no chestnuts roasting when you are
starving
no open fire when you are consistently
cold
I remain suffocating under the
avalanche of your white Christmas.

yOUTh

selfish, absurd, narcissist
boring, obtuse, and negligent
I am a man of twenty years
soon to be twenty-one.

no small time on earth,
but short in the scheme of things.

the purpose of life is to learn
and grow
I question whether I have learned at
all
unable to recall | unable to expand
I question the motive of my existence.

we make what we will of the time given
to us.

shufFLING

It was a cool summer night in the
Windy City.

The streets still lived with the
shuffling souls.

The bars all packed, the union of
voices
a drunken chorus of merriment.

A Dionysian orgy of familiar strangers
and unknown friends.

The sticky sweet smell of rum and
whiskey
engulfed the air and each patron's
breath
was stale with a spittle of hop and
malt.

It was then, as the lights dimmed
that I saw you.

That night in Chicago.

You sat next to me, two stools at the
bar top,
so close we two I could feel the
warmth of
your presence and the lingering scent

of marijuana
on your fingertips.

An intoxicant more compelling than a
siren song
bids me asks your name.

A courage mildly summoned by
inebriation
and sustained through honest interest
a feeling not felt since that night in
Chicago.

MODErn Love

What do you know about your woman?

I'm sure she's pretty for a reason.

She might have all the looks in the
world
but that just ain't enough for me.

I need a woman that speaks
no timid mouse for me
a selfish, directed lady
is all I need.

I know she's spread her love around
I wouldn't have
it any other way
because after she's through
she's back home to stay

Can't tELL

I don't know what the truth is anymore
I can't tell which way's up or down
a melancholy melody
slithers its way all around.

Selfishly sheltered, I keep to myself
a room with a single window, bed, and
TV.

It sure is sad to hear
when that's our best company.

My friends all tell me to break free
but I can't while thoughts of you
are still chained to me.

faiLURE

Sweet is the way life treats me
        just wish it would last
Sweet is the smell of your passing
        please don't walk past
Sweet is the taste of a new day
        but don't eat too fast

Time is a sure thing
        but where do you hide?

Silence is the surest thing
        I've known
Beauty is the greatest thing
        to behold
But trying is the only way
        to never sail
Without fail

ORIGINal Sin

Multiple cycles of life flash by
        before my eyes, inside
        not a bit surprised
by the steady stream of consciousness
that gathers, flows and goes
one message, one symbol, one sign
its meaning elusive, sloppy, selfish,
abusive
by the steady hand that shakes the
cradle
watch as it rocks, but still stable
sweet and savable, newborn babe
lost in a pit of fears, dark, quiet
deadly.
Is she still friendly?
No she won't be, it's been too long
        without being seen, not a one
can come back, obsolete and still
clean.

sWANs

A venereal vaccine
courses through
from the eyes to
the heart
coupling couples
know too true
the madness which starts
passionate embrace,
tender tongues caress
embody the desire
that makes or
breaks the test.

Companionship the
goal,
monogamy of
the soul.

desPair

1990

Anita Hill hearings in U.S. Senate

Clarence Thomas sworn in as SCOTUS justice

Suicide of Kurt Cobain

"Drudge Report" begins

Fox News launched

Defense of Marriage Act

Charlton Heston elected president of the NRA

Columbine High School Shooting

2000

Bush v. Gore US Supreme Court decision

FDA warns Purdue Pharma about OxyContin abuses

Facebook launched

Twitter launched

Virginia Tech massacre

Heath Ledger overdose

Tea Party movement

2010

Aurora, Col. shooting

Sandy Hook elementary school shooting

Mitch McConnell becomes Senate Majority Leader

Orlando night club massacre

Las Vegas shooting

Parkland high school shooting

El Paso shooting

"Unite the Right" White Supremacy Rally

Brett Kavanaugh sworn in as SCOTUS justice

2020

Trump's 'Stop the Steal' insurrection plot unfolds

preCONceptions

Multiple complexes got me stressin'
maladaptive behavior
coupled with a concealed weapon
no knowledge of the event
present,
until it's too late
you're a red dot
and my aim is great.
Slow flows, the post-mortem analysis
but I'm not a bigot
I hold no biases.
I shot straighter than most
to hatred I toast
it leaves me cold
yet secure in my word
and my word unbroken.
Shattering your preconceptions

too SlOW

Murderous masters and militant
blasters can't shatter,
my rhyming bastion
comes crashing down on heads.

Blood spreads
tears are shed
for foolish foes,
couldn't stand these blows.

Mortal men like sloths,
mourn too slow.

It shows.

eScAPiSm

A social escape from the reality that we are not a great progressive society but only one that lives ideally in such fantasy. An ironic twist of the American creed. It is not so lofty a concept since we are masters of escapism. The film industry thrived during the depression, glittering red shoes allowed us to escape the crushing unemployment, the pangs of hunger and want during the depression. Another great war found ourselves engrained in mechanical busy work and nationalistic pride perpetuated onwards until brown and black faces demanded their equal share for their more than equal input and consequences than their brothers and sisters. We deluded ourselves then with concepts of "otherness" and beliefs of superiority in order to escape the truth that we are all one human being behind different eyes and skin tones. Only to find ourselves in another escape through conflict, not domestic but foreign, to bring solidarity, but seeking again to divide. The eighties brought escapism of drug abuse and glorification of the penal laws that still trouble us today, like the

officers that enforce them. We are a
nation of escape. We find ourselves
today lost in world consumption
signifying our relentless wealth and
growth still in a conflict of drugs
and theater dominance. A nation of
escapists of which I am only happy to
be a part of, for better or worse.

paRasITE

An intentional state like weeds in the
grass, vines crisscrossing stone
blocks the very foundation attempting
to become inseparable, but only for a
fleeting moment, easily remedied by a
steady hand.

Drowned by a draught of divine
incarnation, sinfully practiced and
upheld. It shadows and departs as the
sun moves through its celestial course
only to repeat itself time and time
again.

Can a man detach himself from nature?
Only by force of will. The sum of our
nurturing and discovery of self,
without these things our man is lost
only to repeat the mistakes of the
past, dwindling physically like the
last drops of water swirling down the
drain till nothing remains but a
lightly saturated surface a constant
reminder of what was until even that
becomes dry and no trace, no mask is
left of its passing.

A parasite supping on the cocoon of
promises, draining until it becomes a
brittle mass.

VISceral imAGES

A vernacular blacksmith
lyrical bastion
impregnable
to verbal outbursts
and lexical child's play.

I pray thee
beware ye
all who challenge me.

Unstoppable,
a seraphim of the
holy word
a divine tongue
the sporadically spewed
gospel
a maniacal manifesto
mortal testament to
the experience of one
constantly evoking
visceral images
elusive associations
allusions masticated
and spat onto parchment
both effortful and effortless
idle and active consciousness
couple by the chaotic
nature of reality
startlingly
yet rewarding

unfortunately,
lonely.

Words of wisdom
incomprehensible
music carried
to ears that
can't hear.

A silent film

latENT REALiTY

A latent reality
has me trapped in fantasy
subconscious surfing
silently surrounding
dreams, demons
desires, curses
unrepenting heretics in
a sabbath of blood and lust.

The mind an altar
aesthetically pleasant but
spiritually devoid.

Cleaned and kept by
the priest of balance.

Guided by a self-imposed faith
burdened by moral interpretations.

A psyche of past manifested.

intenDEd efFECT

Anxious affliction
medicated necessity
stalwart companion
and my own best enemy
waxing and waning to substance
and drifting amidst tides of
certainty
I'll find you yet at the
bottom of an ocean
no answer within
but the contents of the potion.

Effects so slight they may
be immaterial
but I remember once you
were thought as a miracle
no spectacle, no solution, no
salvation anymore
but your ever-present tantalizing
hooks, I'm caught upon the lure.

All life exists in uncertainty
unaware of our intended effect
we live for reward
and avoid punishment in order to
strive for meaning.

Excessive by nature,
no resources scarce for

America's chosen peoples
no struggle for existence
no reason to cooperate
an uneasy purgatory
of lost desire to ascend
past the mundane.

To truly achieve
self-actualization of spirit.

DEmoCrAcY

Selfish, disservice to mankind.
The subtle tyrant dressed as
savior, with words that bind
as shackles to the spinning
Wheel of Inquisition. No
realization through ignorance,
no victory in strength. All
are pawns in the forward play,
twice forward we thrust ourself
at the mercy of the masters.
Once forward, we exist only as
shields. Our existence transient
yet necessary in their undying legacy.
No scheme greater than fraudulent
existence in servitude. A bondage
more finite than hell itself, as
it relinquishes the one true gift.

free will

all the NOise, NOise, NOise

Callous cawing pervades
surrounding,
filling every orifice
with vile, metallic revulsion.

Pennies in the mouths
of unwanted open ears.

If only Oedipus were deaf

INhERenT

we fall forward
moribund fascination
our surviving trait of experience
amusing how interwoven two
differing aspects of being become
little left of the mold
we shape what we can
firing the kiln of mundane making
selfishly worldly, is there
truly a need?

I'm lost on the inherent meaning

UnfiniShED

Lonesome is the road I am on
ain't no signs or people upon
this lonesome road I travel on
all the traffic is good and gone
and the people can't be found
this lonesome road I travel upon.

All I see is snakes and spiders
sitting silent and spinning webs
all I see is deceptive lies
standing silent with spun webs
waiting with open mouths and traps.

slUm houSe plutocrAcy

Are we man or machine?
Slaves to sensationalism.

Media fiends the tourniquet
tightening the rivers of
sense and rationality, as
we prepare the syringe
of mindless obedience and
        hype.

Injecting the ooze of
nonsensical divinity and
capital gain at
the cost of the
true soul and
conscience of
the American lifeforce.

        We stumble as
        a people,
high on the
plateau of negligence,
nonchalance for our
own impacts on others
as social beings.

We climax as
the world turns
and our bodies turn
blue, the slum house

plutocracy casts out
our body and mind without
a second thought for
        our safety
concerned only for its own.

Our heart beats once to
cry out at the injustice
as we fall dead.

Unwitting serfs to
        the end.

ALl are ONE

Decadently prevalent
Purpose through negligence,
Without providence
Who is profiting.
Salvation like salivation,
A constant unpleasant
Stream,
Speaking words of wisdom
Gutted wisdom
Like unshining
Prisms
Possibly passing
Like time
Between systems
Callously crossing
Between.
The master
The servant
The serf and the lord
All are one in
The same.
Selfishly hoarding
Survival of one
If one is the
Question
Then none
The sum.
Beautiful bastards
Come calling
Wanting

But none shall
Receive
What little they
Leave is
The remnant
Of nothing
But desire
And fire
Of which
Destroys
And burns all
But pyre
And all that
Still stand
Are the
Blasphemies
The sons and
The fathers
Daughters and
Mothers,
Sisters and
Brothers
Leave no one
Unsired.

rEGRESSion

A dastardly bastard
fruitlessly fortunate
and functionally
faster, than
any other master
or callous crafter
of socially intertwined
dreams.

The people are
presently unpleasant
using phrenetic
streams of selfish
misconceptions.

I wouldn't suggest it,
the medicine of the masses
fallen through the
cracks between classes
cautiously aware
of nothing but
disasters
their spirit
lies shattered
as if the
world of
the living
truly mattered.

Brutally battered

the self concept
hit hard
now staggered
not fractured as I
tragically traffic
the means to happiness
through verbal mastery
of concepts, clashing
creeds, stashing seeds
the growth is green
like the grass on
the other side
meant for we.

Beautiful leaves and
sun-tinted trees
the substance of
life of which we
can see
surround yourselves,
regression to
the mean.

ABsence of wORTh

I find myself
once more
in the damned arms
of sanctuary
a constantly pleasant
liquid solace
selfish, yet nurturing.

A solitude from
repugnant dreams,
a self-induced coronary
of which only one cure
exists.

A forthcoming
lie of self-denial
and a blatant dissatisfaction.

Existence is subjective,
a self-emoting stream
of consciousness
with little to no
direction.

Absence of worth is
little more than negligence
of the soul.

There is no self.

Creation in the hands
of few, breeds nothing
more than discrimination
and a loss of focus.

Focus being life's direction,
is a moot point, as life's
twists and turns are the
true reality of existence.

A test of humanity,
a trial of resilience,
and in this case,
a failure of both.

The being of mortality
a constant figure,
but one ignorant
as the grim reaper
has his scythe for
all at neck point
awaiting the doomed failing
of all in the end.

There is none more
sad than the
picturesque, for
a hollow existence
is the saddest form.

A lie constant, that
exists in a perpetual
state of rekindling.

A fire gorged on
timber and broken
delusions.

An individual
removed.

A broken
sad pathetic
being, the love
is lost on this
unique soul.

A craving is
only a temporary
state, lasting briefly yet
lingering in its
tenacity and problematic
in the whole of being.

A manifesto crudely
written and inherently
a poor display of
doubt, repugnance,
revulsion, lasting
hatred of self that
exists only in the
FUCK YOU.

HeAR Me

Can you hear me now?
Through the silence
That abounds.
Lips puckered and
Tongues wag
But no meaning escapes.
Heads, our holy temples,
And ears, their sacred shrines,
Lie desecrated by the times
And lies.

PROblEMS

I can't help but feel inadequate
Unable to cope with the shit
     of today
Drinking and smoking
     problems away
But problems persevere
Harder than stone
Consciously defying growth
A self-imposed ability
     to accept evolution
A slave to the network
A single voice in the universe

nEVer spOKEn

Nothing exists without a reason,
Ramon told himself.
he wasn't sure if
he had said the words aloud or if
they were merely his conscious
consoling him.

He walked from the dilapidated
bus bench, an overused
and never renovated
tan seat covered in
what looked to be
cigarette ash and chewing gum.

After he climbed the steps
into the bus, he
had trouble inserting
his dirty bill into the machine
that seemed to be the only
thing maintained on the bus.

The pudgy driver hit the gas
as he still struggled to shove
his dollar into the shiny
money-taking receptacle.

The driver and the bus
seemed to be one whole entity
as he took up the entire front,
his stubby legs didn't even

move to press the pedal,
it was a movement so minute.

Ramon walked on past all
the old, weary faces,
staring up at him as if
simultaneously asking for company
and shunning him.

Each line in their faces
was a marker for
their own hardships and
seemed like an old song
on the verge of remembrance or
an odd joke on
the tip of the tongue
that's never spoken.

Ramon found an empty seat
in the middle,
where the metal ends and
a strange rubber holds together
the front and the back
so that when it turns
the seats turn
and shudder violently.

Carlisle…San Mateo…Louisiana,
"I wonder how this bus
holds itself together,"
Ramon pondered as
the bus began to turn to
the next stop, Uptown.

promisE

1990

World Wide Web launched

Los Angeles Uprising

Hate Crimes Sentencing Enhancement Act

Ruth Bader Ginsburg sworn in as SCOTUS justice

Violence Against Women Act

Vagina Monologues premieres

Harry Potter and the Philosopher's Stone published

Seattle WTO Protests

2000

A new millennium

Lord of the Rings: Fellowship of the Ring movie released

First legal same-sex marriage in Massachusetts

Howard Dean Chairs DNC and leads 50-State Strategy

Immigration reform protests across US

Obama elected US President

Sonia Sotomayor and Elena Kagan sworn in as SCOTUS justices

2010

Affordable Care Act

Occupy movement

#BlackLivesMatter movement

Boy Scouts of American lifts ban on gay youth

Bernie Sanders historic primary campaign

Hillary Clinton historic presidential campaign

"Year of the Woman"

Green New Deal proposed

2020

Trump impeached first time

tRULy alonE

We can never be truly alone,
despite our feelings towards such,
that is impossible.

All life stems from some form of
contact between one another.

The source continues to elude us but
we strive against the idea that all
that we know and comprehend are the
individuals and beings surrounding
ourselves.

Regardless of creed and recognizing
rational thought, we can't be alone.

PLEthorA

Love, like energy,
cannot be destroyed.

It merely changes form,
becoming something entirely new.

Anger, regret, loathing, sadness
are but a few of the negative
aspects commonly felt.

There can also be serenity,
self-awareness, respect, or humility.

A plethora of states exist through
love.

Love can both damn and save humanity
from itself.

Only time can tell.

unknoWn END

Out of the window
lives await, choices made, streets and
faces walked and met, respectively.

Stirring ever onward into the arms of
experience, for better or worse, we
all take part.

Sun beats down, slowly urinating
yet refreshing as beads of sweat
drip over my eyes bidding
salty farewells as they depart to the
floor.

Perspiration tears that only serve to
remind me of days and nights past.

Aspects of ourselves that fuel
rebirth, is there truly a soul that
lives on, through the disregard of our
mortal selves, living endlessly in the
earth we call home?

Only in the end do we know or find
oblivion. Sweet unknowing bliss.

WatErfALl

I stand upon the mountaintop
the precipice of knowing
the only two options,
failure or success.

Knowledge or death.

I kneel under the waterfall.

Meditate on all things
past, present, future.

The cohesiveness of it all.

That time must always
rapidly thrust forward
only to end in stillness
at the far end of the pool.

impLosION

It is a beautiful evening.

Inebriation, soaking my thoughts
with a lack of responsibility
and the world is once more
my oyster.

The timing is imperfect and the
reasoning is lost in a stagnant sea
of self-pity and destruction.
We mean well.

The fault lines of a planet
shifting and grinding, constantly,
inevitably end in disaster.

Whether it be an eruption
or an earth-shattering throttle
a cathartic release is impending,
in one form or another.

Allow a man to pick his poison,
his soul-scraping sickness and
his heavenly, hell-thrust direction.

Mortal machinations thriving solely
on a mundane moment that passes
as easily as the abruptness of a
sweet song, engrained in memory,
our consequences, life's lessons

to ignore or make sacred.

Is the reality of the situation
much different?

I feel it's not so, as beings
predisposed to creature habits,
we leave things unfinished.

Somewhat in balance
but it is not our fault
this predilection towards
violence of others and the
self.

It is a world
we know best and
cannot help but relieve
ourselves in the alley
of self-denial and imagined
moral righteousness.

So take heart little heathen
and let your sweet majesty
be your undoing.

It is the way of the world
and each gets his
turn as king amongst
the throngs of pawns
who easily outnumber the
bishops, knights, rooks,
and queen.

fRESh EarTh

A rough drag of my cigarette
evokes a wasted future.

Dystopian in nature,
a fate that follows in the
wake of chemical abuse.

Rivers of alcohol,
fields of green
do nothing to alleviate the
weight burdening my mind.

A temporary relief that rises
and falls like the sun.

Obfuscated by the clouds of
my own lack of distress.

Filling slowly with the
rain of self-awareness
falling only with enlightenment.

The wet smell of fresh earth after
a rainstorm.

The scent of rebirth.

inDIStinGUIShablE

I wish to travel
to observe the world
in its most natural form
to fill the plazas of
the world with
my body, among
the thousands like myself.

I want my voice to be
one in unison
indistinguishable from
the bustle of trolleys,
trains, horns, whistles,
the bustle of feet
against the sidewalk.

The chirping of birds,
the cooing of pigeons,
the snow-capped mountains
and the monolithic skyscrapers.

tEMpus fugIT

A founder's sweet curse,
the amalgamation of past, present, and
future.

But all things must end, as
each has its beginning.

Such is the course of life,
in the vast universe of the
dead and the dying.

It is no slight thing that
we as beings thrive so, for
it is struggle that animates
our existence and strengthens
the meaning found in life.

The meaning is subjective,
infinitely numerous in possibility
and practice.

Subjectivity its own reality
whether dynamic or
self-serving, the consequences
of truth, not known until
the end.

A finite end
to all things of time.

radiCAL Mist

Share with me
a delicate masterpiece
mystery
constantly evading me.

The meaning of reality,
        banality,
a serious sort
        of insanity.

Undoubtedly,
I demand a
period of peace
from conscious
thoughts
thick, unclean
like grease.

Please cease
and desist
this radical
mist
constantly clouding
my creativity
surrounding.

sunset ABQ

The land of sunset.

Prismatic purple pink clouds
cross the setting skyline.

Sun-soaked faces fading in
the dawning night.

Eastward
bound, the mountains calling, a
shuffling drunken gait.

drY hEAt

What are the things we want in life?
What drives us to be the beings we
idealize? The things we own are
transitory, the things we value are
part of our belief of self. You can't
change who you are. We can change our
behaviors and how we feel. These
things are not immutable. I need to
leave this place. I need to get away
from the lifeless mesa, the scent of
death that permeates a forgotten and
fallen society of old. My happiness
evaporates like the fallen water in
the desert, present for a brief moment
then gone with little evidence of its
passage. I want life. A city
throbbing, an evident if overlooked
pulse that throngs of inhabitants know
but soon forget. I want to see trees
again. To explore the forests of the
world and to feel rain on my face, to
hear it fall against the roof, and on
the wind. The dryness unending is like
sandpaper against the soul. A rough
grit that shreds away what was once
raw.

DRunken lIoN KING

all souls are connected
life only determined by birth
human parents birth
human children
does the soul fade?
life is secular
pain, love, fear, and
friendship
points on the continuum
of experience
does the soul contain
these imprints of
experience after
death, like
footprints in the
sand or are
they wasted away
by the sea,
reborn to
bear another?

am I as old as
my age or do I
contain the energies of
the ancients, a timeless
vessel of knowledge
traveling through beings, an
eternally recycled
soul wiped clean to seek
some unknown purpose

of life, events in my
lives made evident
through dreams,
experiences emerged
only in a state between
waking and dreaming,
a purgatory of the shared soul
that all know and feel
a spirit realm
of unconscious being,
where knowledge past,
present, and future are
simultaneously known and unknown.

self-awareness, reflection,
and insight makes us unique,
do they really?
can these traits not be generalized to
other lives, other souls?
is it not the nature of being
the need to survive?

to fuck, to fight, to eat, to
shit, to sleep. these are universal
in some form or another, to all life,
are we not just in an animated dream
state, seeking to sleep,
to return to our natural state
of dreaming, to be without life,
to return to the spirit.

or do I simply have too much
time with too much alcohol…

ThROugh THE voiD

I bear witness to the void
my oldest, true friend
the chasm of the self, depreciating
annually
lost amid the mist of imbibed fluids
and ingested substances.

A fog of perception that never truly
clears.

No god to worship, no begotten son to
emulate
only a stark, raving mad reality
of my own making both relieving and
rapist of my own borrowed time.

Would you show me love unkind?

I know no other
a wasted dialogue spoken in separate
tongues.

Yet blissful in knowledge of one's
fate.

Speak now or forever hold your peace.

All tongues remain checked.

The silent revelry of known blasphemy

not wasted on mundane experiences
everlasting
and ever occurring.

A trifle, selfish want in lonesome
wandering
never to feel again, wary of the
warmth within.

Cast upon the self-envisioned chopping
block,
thrown down to the killing floor only
to rise
a masochistic phoenix with broken
wings aflame
in the fires of insecurity and self-
doubt.

i FiNd mYSeLF

I commit to pen and paper,
Obviously inebriated,
And unbecoming to
the truths therein,
but nonetheless true.

I find myself torn
between your happiness
and my own
regret.

the end

Acknowledgements

I'd like to acknowledge my parents first and foremost for instilling a love of language and literature, the intricacies that can be found in spoken and written verse. From my former and at times bleak perspective, my daughter Aurora and her mother helped to bring new hope with vibrancy and unapologetic acceptance. To all the beautiful bastards amidst idle banter and deep cups - caring for my thoughts, gifting their companionship, facing a generation of uncertainty, writing out of weary and angst - I thank you all!